drum star

mmo
5005

You're the soloist with these trio, quartet and quintet groups as they play rock, soul, ballad, jazz, latin and pop renditions of these great songs.

Listen to the recorded drummer. Then add your solo to complete the recording on the version minus drums.

Includes the complete drum charts for all the songs.

★ Feelin' Alright ★
★ One Note Samba ★
★ Misty ★ Getting It Together ★ Oye Como Va
★ I'll Remember April
★ Meditation

5005

COMPACT DISC PAGE AND BAND INFORMATION

MMO CD 5005
MMO Cass. 4074

DRUM STAR

Band No. Complete Version		Band No. Minus Bass	Page No.
1	One Note Samba	9	4
2	Feelin' Alright	10	5
3	Getting It Together	11	6
4	Psychedelic Sally	12	7
5	Meditation	13	8
6	Misty	14	9
7	Oye Como Va	15	10
8	I'll Remember April	16	11

One Note Samba

Music by ANTONIO CARLOS JOBIM
Words by NEWTON MENDONCA

Play 80 bars (two choruses) for flute

D.S. al Coda

Coda

MMO CD 5005
Cassette 4074

4

Feelin' Alright

Words and Music by DAVE MASON

Getting It Together

Words and Music by TERRY PEARCE

Psychedelic Sally

Words and Music by HORACE SILVER

Meditation

Music by Antonio Carlos Jobim
English Words by Norman Gimbel
Original words by Newton Mendonca

MMO CD 5005
Cassette 4074

Misty

Music by ERROLL GARNER
Words by JOHNNY BURKE

Oye Come Va

Words and Music by TITO PUENTE

MMO CD 5005
Cassette 4074

I'll Remember April

Words and Music by DON RAYE, GENE DE PAUL & PAT JOHNSTON

5005

5005

MMO Compact Disc Catalog

BROADWAY

Les Miserables/Phantom of the Opera	MMO CD 1016
Hits of Andrew Lloyd Webber	MMO CD 1054
Guys And Dolls	MMO CD 1067
West Side Story (2 CD Set)	MMO CD 1100
Cabaret (2 CD Set)	MMO CD 1110
Broadway Heroes And Heroines	MMO CD 1121
Camelot	MMO CD 1173
Best of Andrew Lloyd Webber	MMO CD 1130
The Sound of Broadway	MMO CD 1133
Broadway Melodies	MMO CD 1134
Barbra's Broadway	MMO CD 1144
Jekyll & Hyde	MMO CD 1151
Showboat	MMO CD 1160
My Fair Lady (2 CD Set)	MMO CD 1174
Oklahoma!	MMO CD 1175
The Sound of Music	MMO CD 1176
South Pacific	MMO CD 1177
The King And I	MMO CD 1178
Fiddler On The Roof (2 CD Set)	MMO CD 1179
Carousel	MMO CD 1180
Porgy and Bess	MMO CD 1181
The Music Man	MMO CD 1183
Annie Get Your Gun (2 CD Set)	MMO CD 1186
Hello Dolly! (2 CD Set)	MMO CD 1187
Oliver (2 CD Set)	MMO CD 1189
Sunset Boulevard	MMO CD 1193
Grease	MMO CD 1196
Smokey Joe's Cafe	MMO CD 1197

CLARINET

MOZART Concerto, in A	MMO CD 3201
WEBER Concerto No. 1 in Fm, STAMITZ Con. No. 3 in Bb	MMO CD 3202
SPOHR Concerto No. 1 in C Minor Op. 26	MMO CD 3203
WEBER Concerto Op. 26, BEETHOVEN Trio Op. 11	MMO CD 3204
First Chair Clarinet Solos	MMO CD 3205
The Art Of The Solo Clarinet:	MMO CD 3206
MOZART Quintet in A, K.581	MMO CD 3207
BRAHMS Sonatas Op. 120 No. 1 & 2	MMO CD 3208
WEBER Grand Duo Concertant WAGNER Adagio	MMO CD 3209
SCHUMANN Fantasy Op. 73, 3 Romances Op. 94	MMO CD 3210
Easy Clarinet Solos Volume 1 - Student Level	MMO CD 3211
Easy Clarinet Solos Volume 2 - Student Level	MMO CD 3212
Easy Jazz Duets - Student Level	MMO CD 3213
Beginning Contest Solos - Jerome Bunke, Clinician	MMO CD 3221
Beginning Contest Solos - Harold Wright	MMO CD 3222
Intermediate Contest Solos - Stanley Drucker	MMO CD 3223
Intermediate Contest Solos - Jerome Bunke, Clinician	MMO CD 3224
Advanced Contest Solos - Stanley Drucker	MMO CD 3225
Advanced Contest Solos - Harold Wright	MMO CD 3226
Intermediate Contest Solos - Stanley Drucker	MMO CD 3227
Advanced Contest Solos - Stanley Drucker	MMO CD 3228
Advanced Contest Solos - Harold Wright	MMO CD 3229

PIANO

BEETHOVEN Concerto No. 1 in C	MMO CD 3001
BEETHOVEN Concerto No. 2 in Bb	MMO CD 3002
BEETHOVEN Concerto No. 3 in C Minor	MMO CD 3003
BEETHOVEN Concerto No. 4 in G	MMO CD 3004
BEETHOVEN Concerto No. 5 in Eb (2 CD Set)	MMO CD 3005
GRIEG Concerto in A Minor Op.16	MMO CD 3006
RACHMANINOFF Concerto No. 2 in C Minor	MMO CD 3007
SCHUMANN Concerto in A Minor	MMO CD 3008
BRAHMS Concerto No. 1 in D Minor (2 CD Set)	MMO CD 3009
CHOPIN Concerto No. 1 in E Minor Op.11	MMO CD 3010
MENDELSSOHN Concerto No. 1 in G Minor	MMO CD 3011
MOZART Concerto No. 9 in Eb K.271	MMO CD 3012
MOZART Concerto No. 12 in A K.414	MMO CD 3013
MOZART Concerto No. 20 in D Minor K.466	MMO CD 3014
MOZART Concerto No. 23 in A K.488	MMO CD 3015
MOZART Concerto No. 24 in C Minor K.491	MMO CD 3016
MOZART Concerto No. 26 in D K.537, Coronation	MMO CD 3017
MOZART Concerto No. 17 in G K.453	MMO CD 3018
LISZT Concerto No. 1 in Eb, WEBER Op. 79	MMO CD 3019
LISZT Concerto No. 2 in A, Hungarian Fantasia	MMO CD 3020
J.S. BACH Concerto in F Minor, J.C. BACH Con. in Eb	MMO CD 3021
J.S. BACH Concerto in D Minor	MMO CD 3022
HAYDN Concerto in D	MMO CD 3023
HEART OF THE PIANO CONCERTO	MMO CD 3024
THEMES FROM GREAT PIANO CONCERTI	MMO CD 3025
TSCHAIKOVSKY Concerto No. 1 in Bb Minor	MMO CD 3026
Art Of Popular Piano Playing, Vol. 1	MMO CD 3033
Art Of Popular Piano Playing, Vol. 2	MMO CD 3034
'Pop' Piano For Starters	MMO CD 3035

INSTRUCTIONAL METHODS

EVOLUTION OF THE BLUES	MMO CD 7004
The Music Teacher Basic Music Theory	MMO CD 7002
The Art Of Improvisation, Vol. 1	MMO CD 7005
The Art Of Improvisation, Vol. 2	MMO CD 7006

VIOLIN

BRUCH Concerto No. 1 in G Minor Op.26	MMO CD 3100
MENDELSSOHN Concerto in E Minor	MMO CD 3101
TSCHAIKOVSKY Concerto in D Op. 35	MMO CD 3102
BACH Double Concerto in D Minor	MMO CD 3103
BACH Concerto in A Minor, Concerto in E	MMO CD 3104
BACH Brandenburg Concerti Nos. 4 & 5	MMO CD 3105
BACH Brandenburg Concerto No. 2, Triple Concerto	MMO CD 3106
BACH Concerto in Dm, (from Concerto for Harpsichord)	MMO CD 3107
BRAHMS Concerto in D Op. 77	MMO CD 3108
CHAUSSON Poeme, SCHUBERT Rondo	MMO CD 3109
LALO Symphonie Espagnole	MMO CD 3110
MOZART Concerto in D K.218, VIVALDI Con. Am Op.3 No.6	MMO CD 3111
MOZART Concerto in A K. 219	MMO CD 3112
WIENIAWSKI Con. in D, SARASATE Zigeunerweisen	MMO CD 3113
VIOTTI Concerto No.22	MMO CD 3114
BEETHOVEN 2 Romances, Sonata No. 5 in F "Spring Sonata"	MMO CD 3115
SAINT-SAENS Introduction & Rondo, MOZART Serenade K. 204, Adagio K.261	MMO CD 3116
BEETHOVEN Concerto in D Op. 61(2 CD Set)	MMO CD 3117
THE CONCERTMASTER	MMO CD 3118
Air On A G String (Favorite Encores w/Orchestra)	MMO CD 3119
CONCERT PIECES for the Serious Violinist	MMO CD 3120
18TH CENTURY VIOLIN PIECES	MMO CD 3121
ORCHESTRAL FAVORITES - Volume 1 - Easy Level	MMO CD 3122
ORCHESTRAL FAVORITES - Volume 2 - Medium Level	MMO CD 3123
ORCHESTRAL FAVORITES - Volume 3 - Med to Difficult Level	MMO CD 3124
The Three B's-Bach/Beethoven/Brahms	MMO CD 3125
VIVALDI Concerto in A Minor Op.3 No. 6, in D Op. 3 No. 9, Double Concerto Op. 3 No. 8	MMO CD 3126
VIVALDI - THE FOUR SEASONS (2 CD Set)	MMO CD 3127
VIVALDI Con. in Eb Op. 8 No. 5, ALBINONI Con. in A	MMO CD 3128
VIVALDI Concerto. in E Op. 3 No. 12, Concerto in C Op. 8 No. 6 "Il Piacere"	MMO CD 3129
SCHUBERT Three Sonatinas	MMO CD 3130
HAYDN String Quartet Op. 76 No. 1	MMO CD 3131
HAYDN String Quartet Op. 76 No. 2	MMO CD 3132
HAYDN String Quartet Op. 76 No. 3 "Emperor"	MMO CD 3133
HAYDN String Quartet Op. 76 No. 4 "Sunrise"	MMO CD 3134
HAYDN String Quartet Op. 76 No. 5	MMO CD 3135
HAYDN String Quartet Op. 76 No. 6	MMO CD 3136

CELLO

DVORAK Concerto in B Minor Op.104 (2 CD Set)	MMO CD 3701
C. P .E. BACH Concerto in A Minor	MMO CD 3702
BOCCHERINI Concerto in Bb, BRUCH Kol Nidrei	MMO CD 3703
TEN PIECES FOR CELLO	MMO CD 3704
SCHUMANN Concerto in Am & Other Selections	MMO CD 3705
CLAUDE BOLLING Suite For Cello & Jazz Piano Trio	MMO CD 3706

OBOE

ALBINONI Concerti in Bb, Op. 7 No. 3, D Op. 7 No. 6, D Minor Op. 9 No.2	MMO CD 3400
TELEMANN Concerto in Fm, HANDEL Concerto No. 8 in Bb, VIVALDI Concerto No. 9 in Dm	MMO CD 3401
MOZART Quartet in F K. 370, STAMITZ Quartet in F Op. 8 No. 3	MMO CD 3402
BACH Brandenburg Concerto No. 2, Telemann Con. in Am	MMO CD 3403

GUITAR

BOCCHERINI Quintet No. 4 in D "Fandango"	MMO CD 3601
GIULIANI Quintet in A Op. 65	MMO CD 3602
Classical Guitar Duets	MMO CD 3603
Renaissance & Baroque Guitar Duets	MMO CD 3604
Classical & Romantic Guitar Duets	MMO CD 3605
Guitar and Flute Duets Vol. 1	MMO CD 3606
Guitar and Flute Duets Vol. 2	MMO CD 3607
Bluegrass Guitar	MMO CD 3608
George Barnes Guitar Method	MMO CD 3609
How To Play Folk Guitar (2 CD Set)	MMO CD 3610
Favorite Folks Songs For Guitar	MMO CD 3611
Jimmy Raney Guitar Solos	MMO CD 3612
Barnes & Kress Guitar Duets	MMO CD 3613
Play The Blues Guitar	MMO CD 3614

BANJO

Bluegrass Banjo	MMO CD 4401
Play The 5 String Banjo Vol. 1	MMO CD 4402
Play The 5 String Banjo Vol. 2	MMO CD 4403

FLUTE

MOZART Concerto No. 2 in D, QUANTZ Concerto in G	MMO CD 3300
MOZART Concerto in G K. 313	MMO CD 3301
BACH Suite No. 2 in B Minor	MMO CD 3302
BOCCHERINI Concerto in D, VIVALDI Concerto in G Minor "La Notte", MOZART Andante for Strings	MMO CD 3303
HAYDN Divertimento, VIVALDI Concerto in D Op.10 No. 3 "Bullfinch",	

MUSIC MINUS ONE 50 Executive Boulevard • Elmsford New York 10523-1325

MMO CD 5005
Cassette 4074

FREDERICK THE GREAT Concerto in C .... MMO CD 3304
VIVALDI Concerto in F; TELEMANN Concerto in D, LECLAIR,
Concerto in C .... MMO CD 3305
BACH Brandenburg No. 2 in F, HAYDN Concerto in D .... MMO CD 3306
BACH Triple Concerto, VIVALDI Concerto in D Minor .... MMO CD 3307
MOZART Quartet in F, STAMITZ Quartet in F .... MMO CD 3308
HAYDN 4 London Trios for 2 Flutes & Cello .... MMO CD 3309
BACH Brandenburg Concerti Nos. 4 & 5 .... MMO CD 3310
MOZART 3 Flute Quartets in D, A and C .... MMO CD 3311
TELEMANN Suite in A Minor, GLUCK Scene from Orpheo,
PERGOLESI Concerto in G (2 CD Set) .... MMO CD 3312
FLUTE SONG: Easy Familiar Classics .... MMO CD 3313
VIVALDI Concerti In D, G, and F .... MMO CD 3314
VIVALDI Concerti in A Minor, G, and D .... MMO CD 3315
Easy Flute Solos Volume 1 .... MMO CD 3316
Easy Flute Solos Volume 2 .... MMO CD 3317
Easy Jazz Duets for Flute .... MMO CD 3318
Flute and Guitar Duets Vol. 1 .... MMO CD 3319
Flute and Guitar Duets Vol. 2 .... MMO CD 3320
Beginning Contest Solos - Murray Panitz .... MMO CD 3321
Beginning Contest Solos - Donald Peck .... MMO CD 3322
Intermediate Contest Solos - Julius Baker .... MMO CD 3323
Intermediate Contest Solos - Donald Peck .... MMO CD 3324
Advanced Contest Solos - Murray Panitz .... MMO CD 3325
Advanced Contest Solos - Julius Baker .... MMO CD 3326
Intermediate Contest Solos - Donald Peck .... MMO CD 3327
Advanced Contest Solos - Murray Panitz .... MMO CD 3328
Intermediate Contest Solos - Julius Baker .... MMO CD 3329
Beginning Contest Solos - Doriot Anthony Dwyer .... MMO CD 3330
Intermediate Contest Solos - Doriot Anthony Dwyer .... MMO CD 3331
Advanced Contest Solos - Doriot Anthony Dwyer .... MMO CD 3332
First Chair Solos .... MMO CD 3333

RECORDER
Playing The Recorder .... MMO CD 3337
You Can Play The Recorder (Adult) .... MMO CD 3339
Let's Play The Recorder (Children) .... MMO CD 3338

FRENCH HORN
MOZART Concerti No.2 & No.3 in Eb, K. 417 & 447 .... MMO CD 3501
Baroque Brass and Beyond .... MMO CD 3502
Music For Brass Ensemble .... MMO CD 3503
MOZART Sonatas for Two Horns .... MMO CD 3504
Beginning Contest Solos - Mason Jones .... MMO CD 3511
Beginning Contest Solos - Myron Bloom .... MMO CD 3512
Intermediate Contest Solos - Dale Clevenger .... MMO CD 3513
Intermediate Contest Solos - Mason Jones .... MMO CD 3514
Advanced Contest Solos - Myron Bloom .... MMO CD 3515
Advanced Contest Solos - Dale Clevenger .... MMO CD 3516
Intermediate Contest Solos - Mason Jones .... MMO CD 3517
Advanced Contest Solos - Myron Bloom .... MMO CD 3518
Intermediate Contest Solos - Dale Clevenger .... MMO CD 3519

TRUMPET
3 Concerti, Haydn, Telemann, Fasch .... MMO CD 3801
Trumpet Solos Vol. 1 - Student Edition .... MMO CD 3802
Trumpet Solos Vol. 2 - Student Edition .... MMO CD 3803
Easy Jazz Duets for Trumpet .... MMO CD 3804
Music For Brass Ensemble .... MMO CD 3805
First Chair Trumpet Solos .... MMO CD 3806
The Art of the Solo Trumpet .... MMO CD 3807
Baroque Brass and Beyond .... MMO CD 3808
The Arban Duets .... MMO CD 3809
Sousa Marches & Others .... MMO CD 3810
Beginning Contest Solos - Gerard Schwarz .... MMO CD 3811
Beginning Contest Solos - Armando Ghitalla .... MMO CD 3812
Intermediate Contest Solos - Robert Nagel, Soloist .... MMO CD 3813
Intermediate Contest Solos - Gerard Schwarz .... MMO CD 3814
Advanced Contest Solos - Robert Nagel, Soloist .... MMO CD 3815
Advanced Contest Solos - Armando Ghitalla .... MMO CD 3816
Intermediate Contest Solos - Gerard Schwarz .... MMO CD 3817
Advanced Contest Solos - Robert Nagel, Soloist .... MMO CD 3818
Advanced Contest Solos - Armando Ghitalla .... MMO CD 3819
Beginning Contest Solos - Raymond Crisara .... MMO CD 3820
Beginning Contest Solos - Raymond Crisara .... MMO CD 3821
Intermediate Contest Solos - Raymond Crisara .... MMO CD 3822

TROMBONE
Trombone Solos Vol. 1 - Student Edition .... MMO CD 3901
Trombone Solos Vol. 2 - Student Edition .... MMO CD 3902
Easy Jazz Duets for Trombone .... MMO CD 3903
Baroque Brass & Beyond .... MMO CD 3904
Music For Brass Ensemble .... MMO CD 3905
Beginning Contest Solos - Per Brevig .... MMO CD 3911
Beginning Contest Solos - Jay Friedman .... MMO CD 3912
Intermediate Contest Solos - Keith Brown, Professor, Indiana University .... MMO CD 3913
Intermediate Contest Solos - Jay Friedman .... MMO CD 3914
Advanced Contest Solos - Keith Brown, Professor, Indiana University .... MMO CD 3915

Advanced Contest Solos - Per Brevig .... MMO CD 3916
Advanced Contest Solos - Keith Brown, Professor, Indiana University .... MMO CD 3917
Advanced Contest Solos - Jay Friedman .... MMO CD 3918
Advanced Contest Solos - Per Brevig .... MMO CD 3919

DOUBLE BASS
Beginning to Intermediate Contest Solos - David Walter .... MMO CD 4301
Intermediate to Advanced Contest Solos - David Walter .... MMO CD 4302
For Bassists Only, Ken Smith, Soloist .... MMO CD 4303
The Beat Goes On - Jazz- Funk, Latin, Pop-Rock .... MMO CD 4304

TENOR SAX
Tenor Saxophone Solos Vol. 1 - Student Edition .... MMO CD 4201
Tenor Saxophone Solos Vol. 2 - Student Edition .... MMO CD 4202
Easy Jazz Duets for Tenor Saxophone .... MMO CD 4203
For Saxes Only -Arranged by Bob Wilber .... MMO CD 4204

ALTO SAXOPHONE
Alto Saxophone Solos Vol. 1 - Student Edition .... MMO CD 4101
Alto Saxophone Solos Vol. 2 - Student Edition .... MMO CD 4102
Easy Jazz Duets for Alto Saxophone .... MMO CD 4103
For Saxes Only Arranged Bob Wilber .... MMO CD 4104
Beginning Contest Solos - Paul Brodie, Canadian Soloist ... MMO CD 4111
Beginning Contest Solos - Vincent Abato .... MMO CD 4112
Intermediate Contest Solos - Paul Brodie, Canadian Soloist .. MMO CD 4113
Intermediate Contest Solos - Vincent Abato .... MMO CD 4114
Advanced Contest Solos - Paul Brodie, Canadian Soloist ... MMO CD 4115
Advanced Contest Solos - Vincent Abato .... MMO CD 4116
Advanced Contest Solos - Paul Brodie, Canadian Soloist ... MMO CD 4117
Advanced Contest Solos - Vincent Abato .... MMO CD 4118

DRUMS
Modern Jazz Drumming - (2 CD Set) .... MMO CD 5001
For Drummers Only .... MMO CD 5002
Wipe Out .... MMO CD 5003
Sit-In with Jim Chapin .... MMO CD 5004
Classical Percussion, (2CD Set) .... MMO CD 5009
Eight Men In Search of a Drummer .... MMO CD 5010

VOCAL
SCHUBERT German Lieder-High Voice, Vol.1 .... MMO CD 4001
SCHUBERT German Lieder-Low Voice, Vol.1 .... MMO CD 4002
SCHUBERT German Lieder-High Voice, Vol. 2 .... MMO CD 4003
SCHUBERT German Lieder-Low Voice, Vol. 2 .... MMO CD 4004
BRAHMS German Lieder-High Voice .... MMO CD 4005
BRAHMS German Lieder-Low Voice .... MMO CD 4006
Everybody's Favorite Songs-High Voice, Vol.1 .... MMO CD 4007
Everybody's Favorite Songs-Low Voice, Vol.1 .... MMO CD 4008
Everybody's Favorite Songs-High Voice, Vol. 2 .... MMO CD 4009
Everybody's Favorite Songs-Low Voice, Vol. 2 .... MMO CD 4010
17th/18th Cent. Italian Songs-High Voice, Vol.1 .... MMO CD 4011
17th/18th Cent. Italian Songs-Low Voice, Vol.1 .... MMO CD 4012
17th/18th Cent. Italian Songs-High Voice, Vol. 2 .... MMO CD 4013
17th/18th Cent. Italian Songs-Low Voice, Vol. 2 .... MMO CD 4014
Famous Soprano Arias .... MMO CD 4015
Famous Mezzo-Soprano Arias .... MMO CD 4016
Famous Tenor Arias .... MMO CD 4017
Famous Baritone Arias .... MMO CD 4018
Famous Bass Arias .... MMO CD 4019
WOLF German Lieder For High Voice .... MMO CD 4020
WOLF German Lieder For Low Voice .... MMO CD 4021
STRAUSS German Lieder For High Voice .... MMO CD 4022
STRAUSS German Lieder For Low Voice .... MMO CD 4023
SCHUMANN German Lieder For High Voice .... MMO CD 4024
SCHUMANN German Lieder For Low Voice .... MMO CD 4025
MOZART Arias For Soprano .... MMO CD 4026
VERDI Arias For Soprano .... MMO CD 4027
ITALIAN Arias For Soprano .... MMO CD 4028
FRENCH Arias For Soprano .... MMO CD 4029
ORATORIO Arias For Soprano .... MMO CD 4030
ORATORIO Arias For Alto .... MMO CD 4031
ORATORIO Arias For Tenor .... MMO CD 4032
ORATORIO Arias For Bass .... MMO CD 4033
Beginning Soprano Solos - Kate Hurney .... MMO CD 4041
Intermediate Soprano Solos - Kate Hurney .... MMO CD 4042
Beginning Mezzo Soprano Solos - Fay Kittelson .... MMO CD 4043
Interediate Mezzo Soprano Solos - Fay Kittelson .... MMO CD 4044
Advanced Mezzo Soprano Solos - Fay Kittelson .... MMO CD 4045
Beginning Contralto Solos - Carline Ray .... MMO CD 4046
Beginning Tenor Solos - George Shirley .... MMO CD 4047
Intermediate Tenor Solos - George Shirley .... MMO CD 4048
Advanced Tenor Solos - George Shirley .... MMO CD 4049

BASSOON
Solos For The Bassoon Player - Janet Grice, Soloist .... MMO CD 4601

MUSIC MINUS ONE 50 Executive Boulevard • Elmsford New York 10523-1325

drum star

mmo
5005

You're the soloist with these trio, quartet and quintet groups as they play rock, soul, ballad, jazz, latin and pop renditions of these great songs.

Listen to the recorded drummer. Then add your solo to complete the recording on the version minus drums.

Includes the complete drum charts for all the songs.

★ **Feelin' Alright** ★
★ **One Note Samba** ★
Misty ★ **Getting It Together**
★ **I'll Remember April** ★ **Oye Como Va**
★ **Meditation**